Employers are responsible for providing a safe and healthy workplace for their employees. OSHA's role is to promote the safety and health of America's working men and women by setting and enforcing standards; providing training, outreach and education; establishing partnerships; and encouraging continual improvement in workplace safety and health.

This informational booklet provides a general overview of a particular topic related to OSHA standards. It does not alter or determine compliance responsibilities in OSHA standards or the *Occupational Safety and Health Act of 1970*. Because interpretations and enforcement policy may change over time, you should consult current OSHA administrative interpretations and decisions by the Occupational Safety and Health Review Commission and the courts for additional guidance on OSHA compliance requirements.

This information is available to sensory impaired individuals upon request. Voice phone: (202) 693-1999; teletypewriter (TTY) number: (877) 889-5627.

Edwin G. Foulke, Jr.
Assistant Secretary of Labor for
Occupational Safety and Health

# Hazardous Waste Operations and Emergency Response

U.S. Department of Labor

Occupational Safety and Health Administration

OSHA 3114-07R
2008

# Contents

This guidance document is not a standard or regulation, and it creates no new legal obligations. The document is advisory in nature, informational in content, and is intended to assist employers in providing a safe and healthy workplace. The *Occupational Safety and Health Act* requires employers to comply with hazard-specific safety and health standards promulgated by OSHA or by a State with an OSHA-approved State Plan. In addition, pursuant to Section 5(a)(1), the General Duty Clause of the Act, employers must provide their employees with a workplace free from recognized hazards likely to cause death or serious physical harm. Employers can be cited for violating the General Duty Clause if there is a recognized hazard and they do not take reasonable steps to prevent or abate the hazard. However, failure to implement these recommendations is not, in itself, a violation of the General Duty Clause. Citations can only be based on standards, regulations, and the General Duty Clause.

## ACRONYMS

| | |
|---|---|
| BBP | Bloodborne Pathogens |
| CERCLA | Comprehensive Environmental Response, Compensation, and Liability Act of 1980 |
| CESQGs | Conditionally Exempt Small Quantity Generators |
| CFR | Code of Federal Regulations |
| DHS | Department of Homeland Security |
| DOT | Department of Transportation |
| EPA | Environmental Protection Agency |
| ERP | Emergency Response Plan |
| HASP | Health and Safety Plan |
| HAZMAT | Hazardous Materials |
| HAZWOPER | Hazardous Waste Operations and Emergency Response |
| HCS | Hazard Communication Standard |
| ICS | Incident Command System |
| IDLH | Immediately Dangerous to Life or Health |
| MSDS | Material Safety Data Sheet |
| NIMS | National Incident Management System |
| NPL | National Priority List |
| OSHA | Occupational Safety and Health Administration |
| PEL | Permissible Exposure Limit |
| PPE | Personal Protective Equipment |
| RCRA | Resource Conservation and Recovery Act of 1976 |
| SARA | Superfund Amendments and Reauthorization Act of 1986 |
| SCBA | Self-contained breathing apparatus |
| SHARP | Safety and Health Achievement Recognition Program |
| SSP | Skilled Support Personnel |
| TSD | Treatment, Storage, and Disposal |
| TRI | Toxic Release Inventory |
| UST | Underground storage tank |
| VPP | Voluntary Protection Programs |

# Introduction

The dumping of hazardous substances poses a significant threat to the environment. The U.S. Environmental Protection Agency's (EPA) Toxic Release Inventory (TRI) data show that over 18 million tons of hazardous substances covered by TRI were disposed of or released into the environment from 1998 through 2004.[1] Hazardous substances are a serious safety and health problem that continues to endanger human and animal life and environmental quality. Discarded hazardous substances that are toxic, flammable, or corrosive can cause fires, explosions, and pollution of air, water, and land. Unless hazardous substances are properly treated, stored, or disposed of, they will continue to do great harm to living things that contact them, now and in the future.

Because of the seriousness of the safety and health hazards related to hazardous waste operations and emergency response, the Occupational Safety and Health Administration (OSHA) issued its Hazardous Waste Operations and Emergency Response (HAZWOPER) standard, Title 29 *Code of Federal Regulations* (CFR) Parts 1910.120 and 1926.65 (*see* 54 *Federal Register* 9294-9336, March 6, 1989) to protect employees in this environment and to help them handle hazardous substances safely and effectively.

The HAZWOPER standard for the construction industry, 29 CFR 1926.65, is identical to 29 CFR 1910.120. For brevity, the HAZWOPER standard is referenced as 1910.120 throughout the remainder of this publication.

The HAZWOPER standard covers all employers performing the following three general categories of work operations:

- Hazardous waste site cleanup operations [paragraphs (b)-(o)] (e.g., SUPERFUND cleanup),
- Operations involving hazardous waste that are conducted at treatment, storage, and disposal (TSD) facilities [paragraph (p)] (e.g., landfill that accepts hazardous waste), and

[1] U.S. Environmental Protection Agency, TRI 2004 Public Data Release (http://www.epa.gov/tri/tridata/index.htm).

- Emergency response operations involving hazardous substance releases [paragraph (q)] (e.g., chemical spill at a manufacturing plant).

An understanding of how each of these sections are different from each other and what they apply to is essential to ensure compliance with the appropriate section of HAZWOPER. The scope and application [paragraphs (a)(1) and (a)(2)] sections of the standard define these work operations and indicate what sections of the standard they fall under.

State, county, and municipal employees, including hazardous waste treatment, storage and disposal facility employees, and first responders, such as fire and rescue personnel, police, and medical personnel, are covered by HAZWOPER and other regulations issued by the 26 states and territories operating their own OSHA-approved safety and health programs (see listing at the end of this booklet or visit OSHA's website at www.osha.gov). EPA HAZWOPER regulations cover these employees in states without OSHA-approved state plans. The EPA adopted the HAZWOPER standard at 40 CFR Part 311 for public employees (either compensated or non-compensated) who perform operations within the scope of the standard in states that do not have an OSHA-approved state plan.

This booklet provides an overview of the HAZWOPER requirements for each type of work operation and explains each section separately to provide a clearer understanding of the standard. Having this understanding enables employers to protect the health and safety of their employees in these different environments.

## Scope and Application

As briefly discussed in the introduction, HAZWOPER covers three categories of work operations. First, paragraphs (b)-(o) of the standard regulate those operations where employees are engaged in the cleanup of uncontrolled hazardous waste sites. These operations include those hazardous substance operations under the *Comprehensive Environmental Response, Compensation, and Liability Act of 1980* as amended (CERCLA), including initial investigations at CERCLA sites before the presence or absence of hazardous substances has

been determined. Examples of types of uncontrolled hazardous waste sites that would be covered by HAZWOPER include those:

- Listed or proposed for listing on the National Priority List (NPL),
- Listed or proposed for listing on a State priority list,
- Identified or listed by a governmental agency as an uncontrolled hazardous waste site (Note: this includes voluntary cleanup operations), and
- Regulated as a corrective action covered by the *Resource Conservation and Recovery Act* (RCRA).

The second category of work operation is covered by paragraph (p) and includes those employees engaged in operations involving hazardous waste TSD facilities regulated under 40 CFR Parts 264 and 265 pursuant to the RCRA. There are certain types of employers who are exempted from paragraph (p) and these are addressed in the section covering provisions for TSD facilities.

The third and final work operation category is covered by paragraph (q) and includes those employees engaged in emergency response operations for releases of, or substantial threats of releases of, hazardous substances without regard to the location of the hazard. Paragraph (q) also includes provisions for post-emergency response operations, such as performing any necessary cleanup activity. Table 1 provides a summary of the scope and application of the standard, including some example work activities.

| Table 1 – Scope and Application of HAZWOPER | | |
|---|---|---|
| **Work Operation** | **HAZWOPER (Applicable Paragraphs)** | **Examples of Work Activities** |
| **Cleanup Operations**<br>– Cleanup operations required by a governmental body or other operations involving hazardous substances that are conducted at uncontrolled hazardous waste sites.<br>– Corrective actions involving cleanup operations at sites covered by RCRA.<br>– Voluntary cleanup operations at sites recognized by federal, state, local, or other governmental bodies as uncontrolled hazardous waste sites. | 1910.120(b)-(o) | • Site Characterization of Hazardous Waste Site<br>• Drum Removal<br>• Contaminated Soil Removal<br>• Underground Storage Tank (UST) Removal |
| **Operations at TSD Facilities**<br>Operations involving hazardous waste conducted at TSD facilities regulated by 40 CFR 264 and 265 pursuant to RCRA or by agencies under agreement with the EPA to implement RCRA regulations. | 1910.120(p) | • Treating Waste for Disposal at RCRA Landfill<br>• Handling Waste at RCRA Landfill |
| **Emergency Response Operations**<br>Emergency response operations for releases of, or substantial threats of releases of, hazardous substances without regard to the location of the hazards. | 1910.120(q) | • Response to the spill of a highly toxic substance from overturned 55-gallon drum<br>• Response to leaking storage tank<br>• Response to overturned truck carrying hazardous materials<br>• Response to chemical fire |

# Provisions of HAZWOPER for Cleanup Operations

### Safety and Health Program

An effective and comprehensive safety and health program is essential in reducing work-related injuries and illnesses and in maintaining a safe and healthful work environment. The standard, therefore, requires each employer to develop and implement a written safety and health program that identifies, evaluates, and controls safety and health hazards, and provides emergency response procedures for each hazardous waste site. This written program must include specific and detailed information on the following topics:

- An organizational structure,
- A comprehensive workplan,
- A site-specific safety and health plan (often referred to as a health and safety plan or HASP),
- A safety and health training program,
- A medical surveillance program, and
- Standard operating procedures.

The written safety and health program must be periodically updated and made available to all affected employees, contractors, and subcontractors. Necessary coordination between the general program and site-specific activities also should be included in the program. The employer also must inform contractors and subcontractors, or their representatives, of any identifiable safety and health hazards or potential fire or explosion hazards before they enter the worksite.

### Organizational Structure

The organizational structure part of the program establishes the overall chain of command as well as the roles and responsibilities assigned to supervisors and employees. The organizational structure must, at a minimum, include the following elements:

- A general supervisor with the responsibility and authority to direct all hazardous waste site operations,

9

- A site safety and health supervisor who develops and implements the HASP and is responsible for ensuring compliance, and
- The roles and responsibilities of all the other site personnel necessary for hazardous waste site operations.

## Comprehensive Workplan

Planning is the key element in a hazardous waste cleanup program. Proper planning will greatly reduce employee hazards at hazardous waste sites. A workplan should support the overall objectives of the cleanup program and provide procedures for implementation, and incorporate the employer's standard operating procedures for safety and health.

The plan must define the tasks and objectives of site operations as well as the logistics and resources required to fulfill these tasks. For example, the following topics must be addressed:

- The anticipated cleanup and operating procedures,
- A definition of work tasks and objectives, and methods of accomplishment,
- The established personnel requirements for implementing the plan, and
- Procedures for implementing training, informational programs, and medical surveillance requirements.

## Site Characterization and Analysis

Site characterization and analysis is the process of identifying specific site hazards and determining the appropriate safety and health control procedures necessary to protect site employees. The more accurate, detailed, and comprehensive the information available about a site, the more the protective measures can be tailored to the actual hazards that the employees may encounter. At each phase of site characterization, information is obtained and evaluated to define the potential hazards of the site. Much of the information obtained from the initial site characterization is used in the development of the site health and safety plan (HASP) required in 1910.120(b)(4). (Note: the site HASP is addressed further in the next section.)

A preliminary evaluation of the site's characteristics must be performed prior to site entry. A secondary more detailed evaluation must be conducted to further identify existing hazards to aid in the selection of appropriate engineering controls and personal protective equipment (PPE) for future site activities. The evaluation must include all suspected conditions that are immediately dangerous to life or health (IDLH) or that may cause serious harm to employees (e.g., confined space entry, potentially explosive or flammable situations, visible vapor clouds, etc.). As available, the evaluation must include the location and size of the site, site topography, site accessibility by air and roads, pathways for hazardous substances to disperse, a description of employee duties, and the time needed to perform a given task, as well as the present status and capabilities of the emergency response teams.

Additional requirements of the site characterization involve the following:

- PPE to be used during initial site entry,
- Exposure monitoring for ionizing radiation and other IDLH conditions. (Note: An ongoing air monitoring program in accordance with paragraph (h) of HAZWOPER must be implemented after site characterization has determined that it is safe to begin start-up or cleanup operations), and
- Risk identification based on the presence and concentrations of hazardous substances and communication of the risks to those employees who will be working on the site.

## Health and Safety Plan (HASP)

A HASP is a critical program element that aids in eliminating or effectively controlling anticipated safety and health hazards. The HASP must be unique to the site and address all of the elements under paragraph (b)(4)(ii), including:

- Hazard analysis for each site task,
- Employee training,
- Personal protective equipment (PPE) to be used by employees and based on hazard analysis,
- Medical surveillance,

- Exposure monitoring,
- Site control measures,
- Decontamination procedures,
- Emergency response plan,
- Confined space entry procedures, and
- Spill containment.

Although some of the above elements are a part of the overall safety and health program, several others are additional to these elements and are crucial in developing an effective HASP. For example, the task hazard analysis may be the most critical component of the site HASP and addresses the chemical, physical, and biological hazards associated with each particular task or operation and the control procedures that protect employees when they perform that task. Information obtained from the hazard analysis provides the basis for making important decisions regarding the selection of PPE, medical monitoring, exposure monitoring, etc.

It is important to thoroughly address in the HASP how exposure monitoring will be performed as this is necessary for the protection of site employees. Critical information includes the frequency and types of air monitoring, personnel monitoring, environmental sampling techniques and instrumentation including calibration and maintenance methods, as well as the interpretation of monitoring results. For example, there should be established criteria for determining when to upgrade or downgrade PPE based on exposure monitoring results.

Another important element of the HASP is site control, which involves controlling the activities of employees and the movement of equipment which minimizes potential contamination of employees. Site control also protects the general public from site hazards and can prevent trespassing and vandalism. The following information is useful in developing and implementing a site control program: a site map; site work zones; site communication; safe work practices; and the name, location, and phone number of the nearest medical assistance.

The use of a "buddy system" is also required as a protective measure to assist in the rescue of an employee who becomes unconscious, trapped, or seriously disabled on site. In the buddy

system, two employees must keep in visual contact with each other and only one employee should be in a specific dangerous area at any one time, so that if one gets in trouble the second can call for help.

The written HASP must be kept at the site and must always be available for employee, contractor, or subcontractor review. Pre-entry briefings must be conducted prior to site entry and at other times as necessary to ensure that employees are aware of the HASP and its implementation. The employer also must ensure that periodic safety and health inspections are made of the site and that all known deficiencies are corrected prior to work at the site.

OSHA has developed an interactive software program (e-HASP2) that assists employers in developing an appropriate HASP. This eTool integrates decision logic and a large chemical database to assist the user in determining appropriate controls for site health and safety hazards. After site-specific information has been entered, the program generates reports with "model" language that is acceptable to OSHA in preparing a site-specific HASP. This eTool can be found on OSHA's Hazardous Waste web page.

## Safety and Health Training Program

A training program is required under the safety and health program and is also part of the site HASP. This training must be provided to all employees who will work on the site such as equipment operators, general laborers, and supervisors or managers who may have exposure to hazardous substances.

Before performing any work on a hazardous waste site, the employer must provide its employees with initial training based on the tasks and operations that employees will perform and the exposures they are anticipated to experience (see Table 2). Employees who have "equivalent" experience and skills from previous work experience and/or training would not have to receive the initial training provided that the employer can verify it through documentation or certification. Equivalently trained employees who are new to a site must still receive site-specific training before site entry.

Training makes employees aware of the potential hazards they may encounter and provides the necessary knowledge and skills to perform their work with minimal risk to their own, and other employees', safety and health. Both supervisors and employees

must be trained to recognize hazards and to prevent them; to select, care for, and use respirators properly, as well as other types of PPE; to understand engineering controls and their use; to use proper decontamination procedures; to understand the emergency response plan, medical surveillance requirements, confined space entry procedures, spill containment program, and any appropriate work practices. Employees also must know the names of personnel and their alternates responsible for site safety and health. Site personnel who are expected to respond to emergency situations at the site must receive additional training in how to respond to anticipated emergencies (e.g., fires/explosions, hazardous spills, etc.).

| Table 2 – Training Requirements – Hazardous Waste Cleanup Operations | |
|---|---|
| **Workers [1910.120(e)(3)]** | |
| • General site employees (e.g., equipment operators, general laborers, etc.) [1910.120(e)(3)(i)] | 40 hours initial training<br>24 hours supervised field experience<br>8 hours annual refresher |
| • Employees occasionally on site for a limited task (e.g., groundwater monitoring, land surveying, etc.) with minimal exposure [1910.120(e)(3)(ii)] | 24 hours initial training<br>8 hours supervised field experience<br>8 hours annual refresher |
| • Employees regularly on site who are not exposed to health hazards [1910.120(e)(3)(iii)] | 24 hours initial training<br>8 hours supervised field experience<br>8 hours annual refresher |
| • Employees under (e)(3)(ii) or (iii) who become general site workers under (e)(3)(i) [(e)(3)(iv)] | 16 hours of additional training<br>16 hours of additional supervised<br>   field experience |
| **Supervisors/Managers [1910.120(e)(4)]** | |
| • Supervisors of general site employees (e.g., equipment operators, general laborers, etc.) | 40 hours initial training<br>24 hours supervised field experience<br>8 hours of specialized training in employer's<br>   safety and health-related programs<br>8 hours annual refresher |
| • Supervisors of employees occasionally on site for a limited task (e.g., groundwater monitoring, land surveying, etc.) with minimal exposure | 24 hours initial training<br>8 hours supervised field experience<br>8 hours specialized training in employer's<br>   safety and health-related programs<br>8 hours annual refresher |
| • Supervisors of employees regularly on site who are not exposed to health hazards | 24 hours initial training<br>8 hours supervised field experience<br>8 hours specialized training in employer's<br>   safety and health-related programs<br>8 hours annual refresher |

Employees at all sites must not perform any hazardous waste operations unless they have been trained to the level required by their job function and responsibility, and have been certified by a qualified trainer as having completed the necessary training.

Employees who receive the specified training must receive a written certificate upon successful completion of that training. That training need not be repeated if the employee goes to work at a new site; however, the employee must receive the necessary additional site-specific training needed to work safely at the new site. All employees must receive 8 hours of annual refresher training as indicated in Table 2.

It is critically important for a portion of the training program to include hands-on experience and exercises to provide trainees with an opportunity to become familiar with equipment and safe practices in a non-hazardous setting. Traditional hands-on training is the preferred method to ensure that employees are prepared to safely perform these tasks. The purpose of hands-on training, for example, in the donning and doffing of PPE, is twofold: first, to ensure that employees have an opportunity to learn by experience, and second, to assess whether they have mastered the necessary skills.

Note: Non-mandatory Appendices C and E to HAZWOPER provide useful compliance guidelines and assistance in developing a site-specific training curriculum used to meet the training require-ments in paragraph (e) of the standard.

## Medical Surveillance

A medical surveillance program is required under the overall safety and health program and is also part of the site HASP. This program helps to assess and monitor the health and fitness of employees working with hazardous substances. The employer must establish a medical surveillance program for the following:

- All employees exposed or potentially exposed to hazardous substances or health hazards above permissible exposure limits (PELs) (or above published exposure levels if there is no PEL) for more than 30 days per year,

- Employees who wear a respirator for 30 days or more per year on site or as required by 1910.134,

- Employees who are exposed to unexpected or emergency releases of hazardous wastes above exposure limits (without wearing appropriate protective equipment) or who show signs, symptoms, or illness that may have resulted from exposure to hazardous substances, and

- Employees responsible for responding to on-site hazardous materials (HAZMAT) releases (i.e., on-site HAZMAT team).

All examinations must be performed by or under the supervision of a licensed physician, without cost to the employee, without loss of pay, and at a reasonable time and place. Examinations must include a medical and work history with special emphasis on symptoms related to the handling of hazardous substances and health hazards and to fitness for duty, including the ability to wear any required PPE under conditions that may be expected at the worksite. These examinations must be given as follows:

- Prior to job assignment and annually thereafter (or every 2 years if a physician determines that interval is appropriate),

- At the termination of employment or reassignment to an area where medical examinations are not required,[2]

- As soon as possible for employees injured or who become ill from exposure to hazardous substances during an emergency, or who develop signs or symptoms of overexposure from hazardous substances, and

- At more frequent times if the examining physician believes that an increased frequency is medically necessary.

The employer must give the examining physician a copy of the standard and its appendices, a description of the employee's duties relating to his or her exposures, the exposure levels or anticipated exposure levels, a description of any personal protective and respiratory equipment used or to be used, and any information from previous medical examinations. The employer must obtain a written opinion from the physician that contains the results of the medical examination and any detected medical conditions that

[2] If the employee has not had an examination within the last 6 months.

would place the employee at an increased risk from exposure, any recommended limitations on the employee or upon the use of PPE, and a statement that the employee has been informed by the physician of the medical examination. The physician is not to reveal, in the written opinion given to the employer, specific findings or diagnoses unrelated to employment.

Employers should be aware that there are medical surveillance requirements in other OSHA substance-specific standards that may be applicable for individual sites where these hazardous substances are present (e.g., lead, asbestos, and benzene). These substance-specific standards are included under 29 CFR Part 1910 Subpart Z – Toxic and Hazardous Substances.

## Engineering Controls, Work Practices, and PPE

To the extent feasible, the employer must institute engineering controls and work practices to help reduce and maintain employee exposure to or below permissible exposure limits. To the extent this is not feasible, engineering and work practice controls may be sup-plemented with PPE. Examples of suitable and feasible engineering controls include the use of pressurized cabs or control booths on equipment and/or remotely operated material handling equipment. Examples of safe work practices include removing all non-essential employees from potential exposure while opening drums, wetting down dusty operations, and placing employees upwind of potential hazards.

When engineering controls and work practices are not sufficient to reduce employee exposures to or below established exposure limits or are not feasible for site operation, employers must provide employees with and require the use of PPE. The HAZWOPER standard further requires the employer to develop a written PPE program for all employees involved in hazardous waste operations. This program is required under the overall safety and health program and the PPE to be used by employees for each of the site tasks and operations being conducted must be included in the HASP. The PPE program must include an explanation of equipment selection and use, maintenance and storage, decontamination and disposal, training and proper fit, donning and doffing procedures, inspection, in-use monitoring, program evaluation, and equipment limitations.

PPE typically includes respiratory protection, dermal protection (e.g., gloves and protective clothing), eye protection (e.g., safety glasses, goggles, and face shields), and foot protection (e.g., steel-toed boots and chemical-resistant booties). Employers must select and ensure that employees use PPE in accordance with 29 CFR Part 1910, Subpart I. PPE at hazardous waste sites is often identified as a level of protection and frequently referred to as level A, B, C, or D. Non-mandatory Appendix B to HAZWOPER provides guidelines for selecting PPE and further discusses the levels of protection. The bullets below summarize each level of protection.

- Level A provides the greatest level of skin, respiratory, and eye protection (e.g., totally-encapsulating chemical protective suit with self-contained breathing apparatus (SCBA)),

- Level B provides the greatest level of respiratory protection, but a lesser level of skin protection than Level A (e.g., chemical-resistant clothing with SCBA),

- Level C provides skin protection, but a lesser level of respiratory protection than Level B (e.g., chemical-resistant clothing with air-purifying respirator), and

- Level D provides only minimal protection for nuisance contamination only (e.g., general coveralls, hard hat, safety glasses, and boots).

The level of PPE, including the type of material that the components are made from, will depend on the types of hazardous substances present, their concentrations, the physical requirements of the task, the duration of the task, environmental conditions (e.g., heat stress), and the needs of the user (e.g., dexterity). These factors may be different for each site task or operation, which is why HAZWOPER requires that PPE be evaluated for each task and not for the site as a whole. In addition, hazardous conditions can quickly change, requiring a modification (e.g., upgrading or downgrading) to the level and type of PPE to provide the protection needed for the new conditions. For example, a backhoe hitting a pocket of contaminated soil can result in elevated chemical concentrations requiring a possible upgrade to the level of PPE. When conditions exist that create the possibility of immediate death, immediate serious injury or illness, or impairment of escape, employees must be provided with the highest level of PPE. If the hazard is due to a chemical that poses an inhalation hazard, then a positive pressure SCBA or positive pressure air-line respirator must be used. If a chemical poses a severe skin hazard or is highly toxic and can be readily absorbed through the skin, then appropriate protective clothing (e.g., totally-encapsulating suit) must be worn.

In contrast, it is just as important to know when to downgrade the level and type of PPE through exposure monitoring. Wearing too much PPE increases certain hazards such as heat stress, physical and psychological stress, and can impair vision, mobility and communication.

## Exposure Monitoring

Airborne contaminants can present a significant threat to employee safety and health, thus making air monitoring an important component of an effective safety and health program. The employer must conduct monitoring during the initial site entry at uncontrolled hazardous waste sites to identify conditions that are IDLH, exposures over PELs or other published exposure levels, exposures over a radioactive material's dose limits, or other dangerous conditions, such as the presence of flammable atmospheres or oxygen-deficient atmospheres. Accurate information on the identification and quantification of airborne contaminants is useful for the following:

- Indicating work areas and identifying tasks and operations where exposure controls are needed,
- Selecting PPE,
- Assessing the potential health effects of exposure, and
- Determining the need for specific medical monitoring.

After a hazardous waste cleanup operation begins, the employer must periodically monitor those employees who are likely to have higher exposures to determine if they have been exposed to hazardous substances in excess of permissible exposure limits. The employer also must monitor for any potential condition that is IDLH or for exposures over PELs or other published exposure levels since prior monitoring. Situations when periodic monitoring is required include the following:

- Work begins on a different portion of the site,

- New contaminants are being handled,
- Different type of operation is initiated, and
- Handling leaking drums or working in areas with obvious liquid contamination.

## Informational Programs

As part of the overall safety and health program in paragraph (b) of the standard, employers must develop and implement a program that informs employees, contractors, and subcontractors of the nature, level, and degree of exposure from performing hazardous waste cleanup operations (Note: this requirement is typically addressed through initial and refresher training under paragraph (e) of the standard). Those employees who are working outside of the cleanup operations (e.g., clerical staff who work on the periphery of the site) and there is no reasonable possibility for employee exposure to safety or health hazards are not covered by the standard.

## Handling and Labeling Drums and Containers

The handling of hazardous substance-containing drums and containers presents a variety of potential health and safety hazards to employees such as fires/explosions, vapor generation, and physical injury caused by moving heavy containers by hand. As a result, employers must ensure that appropriate methods, procedures, and equipment are in place that address at least the following:

- Drums and containers used during the cleanup must meet the required OSHA, EPA (40 CFR Parts 264-265 and 300), and Department of Transportation (DOT) regulations (49 CFR Parts 171-178), and must be properly inspected and labeled,
- Damaged drums or containers that may rupture or spill when moved must be emptied of their contents using a device classified for the material being transferred, and must be properly discarded,
- In areas where spills, leaks, or ruptures may occur, the employer must furnish employees with salvage drums or containers, an adequate quantity of absorbent material, and approved fire-extinguishing equipment in the event of small fires,

- The employer must inform employees of the appropriate hazard warnings for labeled drums, the removal of soil or coverings, and the dangers of handling unlabeled drums or containers without prior identification of their contents,

- To the extent feasible, the moving of drums or containers must be kept to a minimum, and a program must be implemented to contain and isolate hazardous substances being transferred into drums or containers, and

- Ground penetrating systems or other detection devices must be used to estimate the location and depth of buried drums and containers.

The employer also must ensure that safe work practices are instituted before opening a drum or container. For example, air-line respirators and approved electrical equipment must be protected from possible contamination, and all equipment must be kept behind any existing explosion barrier.[3]

Only tools or equipment that prevent ignition shall be used. All employees not performing the operation shall be located at a safe distance and behind a suitable barrier to protect them from accidental explosions. In addition, standing on or working from drums or containers is prohibited. Special care also must be taken when an employee handles containers of shock-sensitive waste, explosive materials, or laboratory waste packs. When shock-sensitive wastes are handled, the employer must ensure the following:

- Evacuate non-essential employees from the transfer area,

- Protect equipment operators from exploding containers by using a barrier, and

- Make available a continuous means of communication (e.g., suitable radios or telephones), and a distinguishable and distinct alarm system to signal the beginning and end of activities where explosive wastes are handled.

If drums or containers bulge or swell or show crystalline material on the outside, they must not be moved onto or from the site unless appropriate containment procedures have been implemented. In

---

[3] A physical barricade, natural or man-made, that has been designed and constructed of sufficient thickness and density to withstand or deflect the impact loads of an adjacent explosion.

addition, lab packs must be opened only when necessary and only by a qualified person. Prior to shipment to a licensed disposal facility, all drums or containers must be properly labeled and packaged for shipment. Staging areas also must be kept to a minimum and provided with adequate access and exit routes.

## Decontamination Procedures

Decontamination procedures are a component of the site HASP and, consequently, must be developed, communicated to employees, and implemented before employees enter a hazardous waste site. As necessary, the site safety and health officer must require and monitor decontamination of the employee and decontamination or disposal of the employee's clothing and equipment, as well as the substances used for decontamination, before the employee leaves the work area. If an employee's non-impermeable clothing becomes grossly contaminated with hazardous substances, the employee must immediately remove that clothing and take a shower. Impermeable protective clothing must be decontaminated before being removed by the employee.

Protective clothing and equipment must be decontaminated, cleaned, laundered, maintained, or replaced to retain its effectiveness. The employer must inform anyone who launders or cleans such clothing or equipment of the potentially harmful effects of exposure to hazardous substances.

Employees who are required to shower must be provided showers and change rooms that meet the requirements of 29 CFR 1910.141, Subpart J – General Environmental Controls. (Note: HAZWOPER requires showers and change rooms when a hazardous waste cleanup operation will take six months or longer to complete). In addition, unauthorized employees must not remove their protective clothing or equipment from change rooms unless authorized to do so.

Note: Chapter 10 of the Occupational Safety and Health Guidance Manual for Hazardous Waste Site Activities ("4-Agency Manual") provides more information on decontamination procedures; Appendix D of the manual offers example decontamination layouts for levels A, B, and C.

## Hazardous Waste Site Emergency Response

Proper emergency planning and response are important elements of the site HASP that help minimize employee exposure and injury. The standard requires that the employer develop and implement a written emergency response plan to handle possible emergencies before performing hazardous waste site operations. Employers who will evacuate their employees from the worksite location when an emergency occurs and who do not permit any of their employees to assist in handling the emergency are exempt from developing an emergency response plan. These employers must, however, develop an emergency action plan complying with 29 CFR 1910.38 to ensure the safe evacuation of personnel.

Employers that require site personnel to respond to site emergencies must develop a written emergency response plan that includes the following elements:

- Personnel roles, lines of authority, and communication procedures,
- Pre-emergency planning,
- Emergency recognition and prevention,
- Emergency medical and first-aid treatment,
- Methods or procedures for alerting on-site employees,
- Safe distances and places of refuge,
- Site security and control,
- Decontamination procedures,
- Critique of response and follow-up,
- Personal protective and emergency equipment, and
- Evacuation routes and procedures.

In addition to the above requirements, the plan must include site topography, layout, prevailing weather conditions, and procedures for reporting incidents to local, state, and federal government agencies. The procedures must be compatible with and integrated into the disaster, fire, and/or emergency response plans of the site's nearest local, state, and federal agencies.

The plan requirements also must be rehearsed regularly, reviewed periodically, and amended, as necessary, to keep them current with new or changing site conditions or information. A dis-

tinguishable and distinct alarm system must be in operation to notify employees of emergencies. The emergency plan also must be made available for inspection and copying by employees, their representatives, OSHA personnel, and other government agencies with relevant responsibilities.

When deemed necessary, employees must wear a positive-pressure self-contained breathing apparatus or a positive pressure air-line respirator equipped with an escape air supply. In addition, backup and first-aid support personnel must be available for assistance or rescue.

## Sanitation of Temporary Workplaces

Each temporary worksite must have a supply of potable water (suitable for drinking) that is stored in tightly closed and clearly labeled containers and equipped with a tap. Disposable cups and a receptacle for cup disposal also must be provided. The employer also must clearly mark all water outlets that are unsafe for drinking, washing, or cooking. Temporary worksites must be equipped with toilet facilities.

When sleeping quarters are provided, they must be heated. In addition, washing facilities for all employees must be near the worksite, within controlled work zones,[4] and equipped to enable employees to remove hazardous substances. The employer also must ensure that food service facilities are licensed.

## New Technology Programs

New technology for improving the protection of employees on worksites must be evaluated and implemented by employers. Examples of such equipment may include new foams, absorbents, adsorbents, and neutralizers that can be used to decrease the level of exposures to hazardous substances. It is important that new technologies, equipment, or control measures be evaluated by the employer to determine the effectiveness of employee protection before being implemented on site. Manufacturer and supplier information should be reviewed by the employer as part of the evaluation.

[4] A designated work area within the worksite.

# Provisions of HAZWOPER for TSD Facilities

## Safety and Health Program

The standard requires the employer at covered TSD facilities to develop and implement a written safety and health program for employees involved in hazardous waste operations at the facility. The program must be designed to identify, evaluate, and control safety and health hazards in the facility for the purpose of employee protection. It must also include emergency response procedures that meet the requirements of paragraph 1910.120(p)(8), discussed below. Further, the written program must address appropriate site analysis, engineering controls, maximum exposure limits, hazardous waste handling procedures, and uses of new technologies. As conditions or operations change at a TSD facility, reevaluations should be periodically conducted and necessary updates made to the safety and health program.

Note that employers who are conditionally exempt small quantity (hazardous waste) generators (CESQGs) under 40 CFR 261.5 and other (waste) generators who are qualified under 40 CFR 262.34 for exemptions ("excepted employers") do not have to comply with paragraphs (p)(1) – (p)(7), but do have to follow the emergency response provisions under (p)(8). Excepted employers have the option of evacuating their employees from the facility under (p)(8)(i) unless the EPA or a state agency requires that those employees perform emergency response.

## Hazard Communication Program

An effective hazard communication program is a key element required of TSD facilities. The employer must develop a hazard communication program, including providing proper labeling of chemicals, access to material safety data sheets (MSDSs), and appropriate employee training in accordance with OSHA's Hazard Communication standard (HCS), 29 CFR 1910.1200. Hazardous wastes are specifically excluded from the HCS and, therefore, do not have to be included in the TSD's hazard communication program. Other hazardous "non-waste" chemicals to which employees may be exposed at the facility must be included. For example, any neutralizer or other chemical that meets the definition of a hazardous chemical and that is brought on site to

treat or process hazardous waste would be required to be included in the TSD facility's hazard communication program.

## Medical Surveillance, Decontamination, New Technology, and Material Handling Programs

TSD facilities are also required to implement some of the same requirements specified for hazardous waste sites. Paragraph (p) of HAZWOPER references several sections within paragraphs (b)-(o) as follows:

- Medical surveillance program 1910.120(p)(3) references 1910.120(f),
- Decontamination program 1910.120(p)(4) references 1910.120(k),
- New technology program 1910.120(p)(5) references 1910.120(o), and
- Material handling program 1910.120(p)(6) references 1910.120(j)(1)(ii) through (viii), (xi), (j)(3), and (j)(8).

See the discussion of these requirements earlier in this publication.

## Training Program

Employers must develop a training program as part of the overall safety and health program for employees who are exposed to health hazards or hazardous substances at TSD operations. This program must ensure that employees are properly trained to perform their assigned duties and functions in a safe and healthful manner so as not to endanger themselves or other employees.

Paragraph (p)(7) distinguishes between new employees and current employees with respect to required training, as indicated in Table 3. Site personnel who are expected to respond to emergencies at the TSD site must receive additional training. This training is discussed under TSD Facility Emergency Response, below.

| Table 3 – Training Requirements –TSD Facilities | |
|---|---|
| • New employees<br>[1910.120(p)(7)(i)] | 24 hours initial training<br>8 hours annual refresher |
| • Current employees<br>[1910.120(p)(7)(ii)] | Proven previous equivalent training or experience or 24 hours initial training<br>8 hours annual refresher |

Employees must not perform any operations involving exposure to health hazards or hazardous substances at a TSD facility unless they have been trained by a competent trainer to the level required by their job function and responsibility. New employees must also receive a certificate showing that they have completed the necessary training.

## TSD Facility Emergency Response

The standard requires that a TSD facility develop and implement a written emergency response plan in accordance with paragraph (p)(8) as part of their safety and health program to handle possible emergencies at the facility. Employers who will evacuate their employees from the facility when an emergency occurs and who do not permit any of their employees to assist in handling the emergency are exempt from developing an emergency response plan and from the training requirements of paragraph (p)(8). These employers must, however, develop an emergency action plan and ensure that the training of site personnel is consistent with 29 CFR 1910.38.

Employers that require TSD employees to respond to site emergencies must develop a written emergency response plan that includes the following elements:

- Pre-emergency planning and coordination with outside parties,
- Personnel roles, lines of authority, training and communication,
- Emergency recognition and prevention,
- Safe distances and places of refuge,
- Site security and control,
- Evacuation routes and procedures,
- Decontamination procedures,
- Emergency medical treatment and first aid,
- Emergency alerting and response procedures,
- Critique of response and follow-up, and
- PPE and emergency equipment.

If a TSD facility has an emergency response plan required by 40 CFR 264 and 265, containing all of the elements above, a separate written plan will not be required.

The employer must periodically review the facility's emergency response plan and update it as necessary to reflect new or changing site conditions or information.

Employees of TSD facilities who are expected to perform emergency response must be properly trained prior to responding to emergencies. The training must cover the employer's emergency response plan, standard operating procedures, appropriate PPE, and procedures for handling an emergency response. The employer must also document the employee's completion of training or certify the employee's competency.

## Provisions of HAZWOPER for Emergency Response Operations

As previously discussed, paragraph (q) of HAZWOPER applies to releases of, or substantial threats of releases of, hazardous substances without regard to their location. (Note: Except emergency response on hazardous waste sites is covered by paragraph (l) and emergency response on TSD facilities is covered by paragraph (p)(8)). Covered employees generally include first responders, such as HAZMAT team members, fire and rescue personnel, police, and medical personnel who may respond to emergency releases.

Note that paragraph (q) does not apply to "incidental releases" of hazardous substances, which are releases that do not pose a significant safety or health hazard to employees in the immediate vicinity or to the employees cleaning it up. Incidental releases are limited in quantity, exposure potential, or toxicity and present minor safety or health hazards to employees in the immediate work area or those assigned to clean them up. An example may include a laboratory pint-size container that does not pose a significant safety and health threat at that volume. Conversely, a release of chlorine gas above the IDLH level, obscuring visibility and moving through a facility, is an example of a release requiring an emergency response under paragraph (q). In many cases, releases may be incidental or require an emergency response depending on the circumstances of the release (e.g., toxicity and volume of the substance, training and experience of employees in the immediate area, availability of response equipment and PPE, etc.).

## Emergency Response Plan

A written emergency response plan (ERP) must be developed and implemented prior to allowing or permitting an employee response to a hazardous substance release. The plan must cover reasonably anticipated worst-case scenarios. In facilities where the employer has chosen to evacuate employees in the case of an emergency and the employer does not permit any of their employees to assist in handling the emergency, the employer is exempt from paragraph (q) and does not need to develop an emergency response plan. These employers must, however, develop an emergency action plan for the safe evacuation of personnel and ensure that the training of employees is consistent with 29 CFR 1910.38.

Employers that require employees to respond to emergencies must develop a written emergency response plan that includes the following elements:

- Pre-emergency planning and coordination with outside parties,
- Personnel roles, lines of authority, training, and communication,
- Emergency recognition and prevention,
- Safe distances and places of refuge,
- Site security and control,
- Evacuation routes and procedures,
- Decontamination,
- Emergency medical treatment and first aid,
- Emergency alerting and response procedures,
- Critique of response and follow-up, and
- PPE and emergency equipment.

Employers may use the local emergency response plan, or the state emergency response plan, if the above elements are covered, as part of their emergency response plan. Those items of the local and/or state emergency response plans that are addressed by Title III of the *Superfund Amendments and Reauthorization Act of 1986* (SARA) may be included in the employer's emergency plan for the employer's and employees' use.

## Procedures for Handling an Emergency Response

HAZWOPER requires the implementation of an incident command system (ICS) for responses to an emergency release of hazardous

substances. The ICS is a widely accepted approach to effectively organize, control, and manage operations at an emergency incident. The individual in charge of the ICS is the senior official responding to the incident who oversees the coordination, direction, and actions of the response operations. All site communications are routed through the ICS and the senior official. Ultimately, the implementation of the ICS helps to reduce confusion, improve safety, organize and coordinate actions, and facilitates the effective management of the incident.

Compliance with the ICS, as defined by the National Incident Management System (NIMS), is consistent with compliance with using an ICS under this section of HAZWOPER. NIMS was published by the Department of Homeland Security (DHS) on March 1, 2004. The NIMS provides a consistent nationwide template for incident management that allows responders to work together more effectively. The NIMS adopts the ICS, including operating characteristics, interactive management components, and structure of incident management and emergency response organizations engaged throughout the life cycle of an incident.

The standard requires additional specific procedures for response operations. It requires the individual in charge (i.e., Incident Commander) of the ICS to evaluate site conditions and implement appropriate response operations, hazard controls, and PPE. A safety officer must be designated to provide direction and assistance to ensure the safety of response operations. It also requires that personnel in the area of the incident and related hazards be limited to those actively performing emergency response operations and that backup personnel stand by with appropriate equipment to provide assistance or rescue.

## Training

Emergency responders must be trained prior to their participation in emergency response operations and their training must be based on the functions and duties the responders will be expected to perform. For example, if an employee is simply expected to notify the emergency response team upon discovery of an emergency release and evacuate from the area, the employee would be trained to the first responder awareness level; or if an employee who is responding initially in a defensive manner for the purpose of protecting nearby persons, property, or the environment from the

effects of the release, but does not approach the point of release, the employee would be trained to the first responder operations level. If, however, the employee is expected to approach the point of release for the purpose of stopping the release, the employee would minimally need to be trained to the HAZMAT technician level. If an employee is expected to have more direct and specific knowledge of the various hazardous substances and to assist the HAZMAT technician in the response, the employee would minimally need to be trained to the HAZMAT specialist level. Consequently, employers must evaluate the roles and tasks that employees will perform and train them appropriately.

In addition to the training levels established in the standard for emergency responders, two additional personnel classifications are provided: skilled support personnel (SSP) and specialist employees. SSP are employees who are needed to temporarily perform immediate emergency support work (e.g., excavator operators). SSP must be provided an initial site briefing covering PPE use, the chemical hazards involved, and the tasks to be performed. Specialist employees are those who, in the course of their regular job duties, work with and are trained in the hazards of specific hazardous substances. They may be called upon to provide technical advice or assistance at a hazardous substance release incident.

SSP and specialist employees are covered in paragraphs (q)(4) and (q)(5) of HAZWOPER. Required training and competencies for emergency responders is covered in paragraph (q)(6) and trainer qualifications is covered in paragraph (q)(7). Refresher training is covered in paragraph (q)(8) of the standard (see Table 4).

Trainers who teach any of the training subjects must have either completed a training course on the subjects they are expected to

| Table 4 – Training Requirements – Emergency Response Operations | |
|---|---|
| **Emergency Responders [1910.120(q)(6)]** | |
| • First Responder Awareness Level (Witnesses or discovers a release of hazardous substances and is trained to notify the proper authorities) | Sufficient initial training and competencies<br>Annual refresher |
| • First Responder Operations Level (Responds to the releases of hazardous substances in a defensive manner, without trying to stop the release) | 8 hours initial training and competencies<br>Annual refresher |

31

| | |
|---|---|
| • Hazardous Materials Technician (Responds aggressively to stop the release of hazardous substances) | 24 hours initial training and competencies Annual refresher |
| • Hazardous Materials Specialist (Responds with and in support of HAZMAT technicians, but who have specific knowledge of various hazardous substances) | 24 hours initial training and competencies Annual refresher |
| • On Scene Incident Commander (Assumes control of the incident scene beyond the first responder awareness level) | 24 hours initial training and competencies Annual refresher |
| **Other Employees [1910.120(q)(4)-(q)(5)]** | |
| • Skilled Support Personnel (temporarily perform immediate emergency support work) | Safety and health briefing at response site |
| • Specialist Employees (provide technical advice/assistance on specific hazardous substances) | Annual demonstration of specialized competencies |

teach or they must have the training and/or academic credentials and instructional experience to demonstrate competent teaching skills. In addition, employees need not necessarily receive a certificate, but the employer must certify training with some form of documentation. (Note: the HAZWOPER standard does not contain a specific certification requirement for Awareness Level training). It is considered good practice to provide employees with a training certificate as well as to document the training in the employer's records. The employer also must document in its ERP its training plan for personnel who respond to hazardous substance incidents.

## Medical Surveillance

Members of organized and designated HAZMAT teams and HAZMAT specialists must receive a baseline physical examination and medical surveillance in accordance with 1910.120(f). (Note: see the previous discussion on medical surveillance at 1910.120(f)). The examinations must be provided prior to initial assignment, at least yearly thereafter, and at termination of employment. The medical examination must include a medical and work history with the actual content of medical examinations to be determined by the attending physician.

Medical consultations must also be provided in cases where employees are injured or develop signs or symptoms of overexposure to health hazards. Consultations must be provided as soon as possible following an incident, and also at additional times if the physician determines that it is necessary. Similar to examinations, the content of consultations is determined by the attending physician.

## PPE

Designated HAZMAT team members and hazardous materials specialists must be provided with the appropriate protective clothing and other necessary equipment. Furthermore, employers must ensure that paragraphs (g)(3)-(g)(5) of HAZWOPER are followed, which cover the requirements for PPE selection, totally-encapsulating chemical protective suits, and the PPE program. (Note: see the previous discussion on PPE at 1910.120(g)).

### Post-Emergency Response Operations

After an emergency release, it is often necessary to transition from an emergency response operation to a hazardous substances cleanup operation. In such cases, post-emergency cleanup begins when the individual in charge of the emergency response declares the site to be under control and ready for cleanup. The post-emergency cleanup can be performed by two basic groups of employees: employees of the site where the emergency release occurred or employees from off the site.

Employees of the site who perform post-emergency cleanup on plant property are employees that are typically more familiar with the types of hazardous substances of the site, site conditions, and methods to appropriately protect themselves from the related hazards. As a result, these employees do not need to be trained in accordance with 1910.120(e). However, these employees do have to complete the training required by 1910.38, 1910.134, 1910.1200, and other appropriate safety and health training made necessary by the tasks they are expected to perform during the cleanup.

Employees who do not work at the facility where the release occurred, and who arrive after the emergency is declared to be over, must meet the requirements of 1910.120(b)-(o) and be trained in accordance with 1910.120(e). In other words, their participation in

the post-emergency cleanup is to be treated as hazardous waste site cleanup operations as discussed earlier in this publication. The HAZWOPER standard does, however, allow emergency responders, trained in accordance with 1910.120(q)(6), who took part in the initial emergency response to continue working through the cleanup operation without any additional training.

# Related Requirements

### Recordkeeping

In 1988, OSHA revised the standard requiring employers to provide employees with information to assist in the management of their own safety and health. The standard, Access to Employee Exposure and Medical Records (29 CFR 1910.1020), permits direct access to these records by employees exposed to hazardous materials, or by their designated representatives, and by OSHA.

The employer must keep exposure records for 30 years and medical records for at least the duration of employment plus 30 years. Records of employees who have worked for less than 1 year need not be retained after employment, but the employer must provide these records to the employee upon termination of employment. First-aid records of one-time treatment need not be retained for any specified period. Employers should be aware that OSHA's substance-specific standards under 29 CFR Part 1910 Subpart Z – Toxic and Hazardous Substances may have their own record-retention requirements and these would take precedence over 1910.1020.

The employer must inform each employee of the existence, location, and availability of these records. Whenever an employer plans to stop doing business and there is no successor employer to receive and maintain these records, the employer must notify employees of their right to access these records at least 3 months before the employer ceases to do business. At the same time, employers also must notify the National Institute for Occupational Safety and Health.

Under paragraph (f)(8) of HAZWOPER, at a minimum, medical records must include the following information:

- Employee's name and social security number,

- Physicians' written opinions,
- Employee's medical complaints related to exposure to hazardous substances, and
- Information provided to the treating physician.

## Hazard Communication Standard (HCS)

Title III of SARA requires employers covered by the Hazard Communication standard (29 CFR 1910.1200) to maintain material safety data sheets (MSDSs) and submit such information to state emergency response commissions, local emergency planning committees, and the local fire department. Under this requirement, employers covered by HCS must provide chemical hazard information to both employees and surrounding communities. Consequently, in the case of an emergency response to hazardous substances at a site, the local fire department may already be aware of the chemicals present at the site since data may have been provided through MSDSs.

## Bloodborne Pathogens Standard (BBP)

The Bloodborne Pathogens standard (29 CFR 1910.1030) may interface with HAZWOPER in several scenarios, including, but not limited to, cleanup of a hazardous waste site containing infectious waste, operation of a RCRA-permitted incinerator that burns infectious waste, and response to an emergency caused by the uncontrolled release of infectious waste or where infectious waste is part of the release.

A specific example includes first-aid providers on a hazardous waste site who are expected to treat injured employees. Because these personnel have an anticipated exposure to blood or other potentially infectious materials, they would fall under the scope of the standard. (Note: other potentially infectious materials is defined in paragraph (b) of the BBP standard.)

Some basic requirements of the BBP standard include:

- A written exposure control plan, to be updated annually,
- Use of universal precautions,
- Consideration, implementation, and use of safer needle devices,

- Use of engineering and work practice controls and appropriate PPE (e.g., gloves, face and eye protection, gowns, etc.),
- Hepatitis B vaccination provided to exposed employees at no cost,
- Medical follow-up in the event of an "exposure incident,"
- Use of labels or color-coding for items such as sharps disposal containers and containers for regulated waste, contaminated laundry, and certain specimens,
- Employee training, and
- Proper containment of all sharps and regulated waste.

## Other OSHA Standards

In addition to the related OSHA standards above, there are many other OSHA standards that can interface with HAZWOPER depending on the specific hazards on the site and the types of work being performed. A few of these other standards may include:

- 29 CFR 1910.146 (Permit-Required Confined Spaces),
- 29 CFR 1910.147 (Control of Hazardous Energy [Lockout/Tagout]),
- 29 CFR Part 1910 Subpart Z (Toxic and Hazardous Substances), and
- 29 CFR Part 1926 Subpart P (Excavations)

## Other Resources

- OSHA, Hazardous Waste Safety and Health Topics web page, http://www.osha.gov/SLTC/hazardouswaste/index.html;
- OSHA, Emergency Preparedness and Response Safety and Health Topics webpage, http://www.osha.gov/SLTC/emergencypreparedness/index.html;
- OSHA, Brownfields Safety and Health Topics webpage, http://www.osha.gov/SLTC/brownfields/index.html;
- OSHA, e-HASP2 eTool, http://www.osha.gov/dep/etools/ehasp/index.html;
- OSHA, Occupational Safety and Health Guidance Manual for Hazardous Waste Site Activities ("4-Agency Manual"),

http://www.osha.gov/Publications/complinks/OSHG-HazWaste/4agency.html; and

- OSHA, ICS eTool, http://www.osha.gov/SLTC/etools/ics/index.html.

## Summary

Hazardous substances, when not handled properly, can pose a significant health and safety risk to employees. OSHA recognizes the need to protect the health and safety of employees who are exposed to these substances and work on hazardous waste sites or at TSD facilities, and who perform emergency response. The HAZWOPER standard provides employers and employees with the information and training criteria necessary to improve workplace health and safety, thereby reducing the number of injuries and illnesses resulting from exposure to hazardous substances. To effectively protect the health and safety of employees, it is critical that employers understand the scope and application of the standard and can determine which sections apply to their specific scenario. For example, hazards generated from an explosion at a chemical plant are very different from those existing on a hazardous waste site where site conditions are more controlled and hazards have been more fully identified. The purpose of this publication is to provide an understanding of how HAZWOPER applies to different work environments, and to address the related requirements for those worksites.

---

# OSHA Assistance

---

OSHA can provide extensive help through a variety of programs, including technical assistance about effective safety and health programs, state plans, workplace consultations, voluntary protection programs, strategic partnerships, training and education, and more. An overall commitment to workplace safety and health can add value to your business, to your workplace, and to your life.

### Safety and Health Program Management Guidelines

Effective management of employee safety and health protection is a decisive factor in reducing the extent and severity of work-related injuries and illnesses and their related costs. In fact, an effective safety and health program forms the basis of good employee protection, can save time and money, increase productivity and reduce employee injuries, illnesses, and related workers' compensation costs.

To assist employers and employees in developing effective safety and health programs, OSHA published recommended Safety and Health Program Management Guidelines (54 *Federal Register* (16): 3904-3916, January 26, 1989). These voluntary guidelines can be applied to all places of employment covered by OSHA.

The guidelines identify four general elements critical to the development of a successful safety and health management system:

- Management leadership and employee involvement,
- Worksite analysis,
- Hazard prevention and control, and
- Safety and health training.

The guidelines recommend specific actions, under each of these general elements, to achieve an effective safety and health program. The *Federal Register* notice is available online at www.osha.gov.

### State Programs

*The Occupational Safety and Health Act of 1970* (OSH Act) encourages states to develop and operate their own job safety and

health plans. OSHA approves and monitors these plans. Twenty-four states, Puerto Rico, and the Virgin Islands currently operate approved state plans: 22 cover both private and public (state and local government) employment; Connecticut, New Jersey, New York, and the Virgin Islands cover the public sector only. States and territories with their own OSHA-approved occupational safety and health plans must adopt standards identical to, or at least as effective as, the Federal OSHA standards.

## Consultation Services

Consultation assistance is available on request to employers who want help in establishing and maintaining a safe and healthful workplace. Largely funded by OSHA, the service is provided at no cost to the employer. Primarily developed for smaller employers with more hazardous operations, the consultation service is delivered by state governments employing professional safety and health consultants. Comprehensive assistance includes an appraisal of all mechanical systems, work practices, and occupational safety and health hazards of the workplace and all aspects of the employer's present job safety and health program. In addition, the service offers assistance to employers in developing and implementing an effective safety and health program. No penalties are proposed or citations issued for hazards identified by the consultant. OSHA provides consultation assistance to the employer with the assurance that his or her name and firm and any information about the workplace will not be routinely reported to OSHA enforcement staff.

Under the consultation program, certain exemplary employers may request participation in OSHA's Safety and Health Achievement Recognition Program (SHARP). Eligibility for participation in SHARP includes receiving a comprehensive consultation visit, demonstrating exemplary achievements in workplace safety and health by abating all identified hazards, and developing an excellent safety and health program.

Employers accepted into SHARP may receive an exemption from programmed inspections (not complaint or accident investigation inspections) for a period of 1 year. For more information concerning consultation assistance, see OSHA's website at www.osha.gov.

### Voluntary Protection Programs (VPP)

Voluntary Protection Programs and on-site consultation services, when coupled with an effective enforcement program, expand employee protection to help meet the goals of the OSH Act. The VPPs motivate others to achieve excellent safety and health results in the same outstanding way as they establish a cooperative relationship between employers, employees, and OSHA.

For additional information on VPP and how to apply, contact the OSHA regional offices listed at the end of this publication.

### Strategic Partnership Program

OSHA's Strategic Partnership Program, the newest member of OSHA's cooperative programs, helps encourage, assist, and recognize the efforts of partners to eliminate serious workplace hazards and achieve a high level of employee safety and health. Whereas OSHA's Consultation Program and VPP entail one-on-one relationships between OSHA and individual worksites, most strategic partnerships seek to have a broader impact by building cooperative relationships with groups of employers and employees. These partnerships are voluntary, cooperative relationships between OSHA, employers, employee representatives, and others (e.g., trade unions, trade and professional associations, universities, and other government agencies).

For more information on this and other cooperative programs, contact your nearest OSHA office, or visit OSHA's website at www.osha.gov.

### Alliance Program

Through the Alliance Program, OSHA works with groups committed to safety and health, including businesses, trade or professional organizations, unions and educational institutions, to leverage resources and expertise to develop compliance assistance tools and resources and share information with employers and employees to help prevent injuries, illnesses and fatalities in the workplace.

Alliance program agreements have been established with a wide variety of industries including meat, apparel, poultry, steel, plastics, maritime, printing, chemical, construction, paper and telecommunications. These agreements are addressing many safety and health

hazards and at-risk audiences, including silica, fall protection, amputations, immigrant workers, youth and small businesses. By meeting the goals of the Alliance Program agreements (training and education, outreach and communication, and promoting the national dialogue on workplace safety and health), OSHA and the Alliance Program participants are developing and disseminating compliance assistance information and resources for employers and employees such as electronic assistance tools, fact sheets, toolbox talks, and training programs.

## OSHA Training and Education

OSHA area offices offer a variety of information services, such as compliance assistance, technical advice, publications, audiovisual aids, and speakers for special engagements. OSHA's Training Institute in Arlington Heights, IL, provides basic and advanced courses in safety and health for Federal and state compliance officers, state consultants, Federal agency personnel, and private sector employers, employees, and their representatives.

The OSHA Training Institute also has established OSHA Training Institute Education Centers to address the increased demand for its courses from the private sector and from other federal agencies. These centers include colleges, universities, and nonprofit training organizations that have been selected after a competition for partic-ipation in the program.

OSHA also provides funds to nonprofit organizations, through grants, to conduct workplace training and education in subjects where OSHA believes there is a lack of workplace training. Grants are awarded annually.  Grant recipients are expected to contribute 20 percent of the total grant cost.

For more information on training and education, contact the OSHA Training Institute, Directorate of Training and Education, 2020 South Arlington Heights Road, Arlington Heights, IL, 60005, (847) 297-4810, or see Training on OSHA's website at www.osha.gov. For further information on any OSHA program, contact your nearest OSHA regional office listed at the end of this publication.

## Information Available Electronically

OSHA has a variety of materials and tools available on its website at www.osha.gov. These include electronic compliance assistance

tools, such as *Safety and Health Topics Pages, eTools, Expert Advisors;* regulations, directives, publications and videos; and other information for employers and employees. OSHA's software programs and compliance assistance tools walk you through challenging safety and health issues and common problems to find the best solutions for your workplace.

A wide variety of OSHA materials, including standards, interpretations, directives, and more can be purchased on CD-ROM from the U.S. Government Printing Office, Superintendent of Documents, toll-free phone (866) 512-1800.

## OSHA Publications

OSHA has an extensive publications program. For a listing of free items, visit OSHA's website at www.osha.gov or contact the OSHA Publications Office, U.S. Department of Labor, 200 Constitution Avenue, NW, N-3101, Washington, DC 20210; telephone (202) 693-1888 or fax to (202) 693-2498.

## Contacting OSHA

To report an emergency, file a complaint, or seek OSHA advice, assistance, or products, call (800) 321-OSHA or contact your nearest OSHA Regional office listed at the end of this publication. The teletypewriter (TTY) number is (877) 889-5627.

Written correspondence can be mailed to the nearest OSHA Regional or Area Office listed at the end of this publication or to OSHA's national office at: U.S. Department of Labor, Occupational Safety and Health Administration, 200 Constitution Avenue, N.W., Washington, DC 20210.

By visiting OSHA's website at www.osha.gov, you can also:

- File a complaint online,
- Submit general inquiries about workplace safety and health electronically, and
- Find more information about OSHA and occupational safety and health.

# OSHA Regional Offices

**Region I**
(CT,* ME, MA, NH, RI, VT*)
JFK Federal Building, Room E340
Boston, MA 02203
(617) 565-9860

**Region II**
(NJ,* NY,* PR,* VI*)
201 Varick Street, Room 670
New York, NY 10014
(212) 337-2378

**Region III**
(DE, DC, MD,* PA, VA,* WV)
The Curtis Center
170 S. Independence Mall West
Suite 740 West
Philadelphia, PA 19106-3309
(215) 861-4900

**Region IV**
(AL, FL, GA, KY,* MS, NC,* SC,* TN*)
61 Forsyth Street, SW, Room 6T50
Atlanta, GA 30303
(404) 562-2300

**Region V**
(IL, IN,* MI,* MN,* OH, WI)
230 South Dearborn Street
Room 3244
Chicago, IL 60604
(312) 353-2220

**Region VI**
(AR, LA, NM,* OK, TX)
525 Griffin Street, Room 602
Dallas, TX 75202
(972) 850-4145

**Region VII**
(IA,* KS, MO, NE)
Two Pershing Square
2300 Main Street, Suite 1010
Kansas City, MO 64108-2416
(816) 283-8745

**Region VIII**
(CO, MT, NO, SO, UT,* WY*)
1999 Broadway, Suite 1690
PO Box 46550
Denver, CO 80202-5716
(720) 264-6550

**Region IX**
(AZ,* CA,* HI,* NV,* and American
Samoa, Guam and the Northern
Mariana Islands)
90 7th Street, Suite 18-100
San Francisco, CA 94103
(415) 625-2547

**Region X**
(AK,* ID, OR,* WA*)
1111 Third Avenue, Suite 715
Seattle, WA 98101-3212
(206) 553-5930

* These states and territories operate their own OSHA-approved job safety and health programs and cover state and local government employees as well as private sector employees. The Connecticut, New Jersey, New York and Virgin Islands plans cover public employees only. States with approved programs must have standards that are identical to, or at least as effective as, the Federal OSHA standards.

**Note:** To get contact information for OSHA Area Offices, OSHA-approved State Plans and OSHA Consultation Projects, please visit us online at www.osha.gov or call us at 1-800-321-0SHA.

www.ingramcontent.com/pod-product-compliance
Lightning Source LLC
Chambersburg PA
CBHW051823170526
45167CB00005B/2129